My OXFORD
ABC and 123
Picture Rhyme Book

With rhymes by
Roger McGough

Illustrated by
Debi Gliori

Compiled by
Dee Reid and **Nicholas Tucker**

Hello

Goodbye

Pretty boy

OXFORD
UNIVERSITY PRESS

OXFORD
UNIVERSITY PRESS

Great Clarendon Street, Oxford OX2 6DP

Oxford University Press is a department of the University of Oxford.
It furthers the University's objective of excellence in research, scholarship,
and education by publishing worldwide in

Oxford   New York

Athens   Auckland   Bangkok   Bogotá Buenos Aires   Calcutta
Cape Town   Chennai   Dar es Salaam   Delhi Florence   Hong Kong   Istanbul
Karachi   Kuala Lumpur   Madrid Melbourne   Mexico City   Mumbai
Nairobi   Paris   São Paulo   Singapore   Taipei   Tokyo   Toronto   Warsaw
with associated companies in Berlin Ibadan

Oxford is a registered trade mark of Oxford University Press
in the UK and certain other countries

Word Rhymes © Roger McGough 1990
Number Rhymes © Roger McGough 1992
ABC Text © Dee Reid 1990
123 Text © Nicholas Tucker 1992
ABC Illustrations © Oxford University Press
123 Illustrations © Debi Gliori 1992

The moral rights of the authors/illustrator has been asserted

First published seperately as *The Oxford ABC Picture Dictionary* 1990
and *My Oxford 123 Book of Number Rhymes* 1992 and
My Oxford 123 Number Rhyme Book 1994
This edition published 1999

British Library Cataloguing in Publication Data available

ISBN 0-19-910588-X

3 5 7 9 10 8 6 4 2

Printed in Hong Kong

ABC Parents' notes

This fun-filled activity dictionary has so much to keep children amused while they are learning.

Each double page has a beautifully illustrated picture packed full of items beginning with the same letter of the alphabet. There is a wealth of detail for readers of all ages to pore over. Each page also has a puzzle activity, a joke and some silhouettes to identify.

The dictionary entries each have their own little picture and an accompanying phrase or rhyme. These have been devised to cater for children's fascination with the sounds that words make.

Children will enjoy getting their tongues round the humorous verses and this playing with rhyme is the perfect preparation for becoming a reader.

Younger children will enjoy finding the ten listed items in the busy large picture. Older children (and adults!) might like to search to find the many extra items that begin with each particular letter. You will find a checklist of the illustrated items at the back of the book. This book can be dipped into and enjoyed on many occasions and in many ways. It offers an early introduction to alphabet order and a delightful means of expanding a child's vocabulary.

Dee Reid

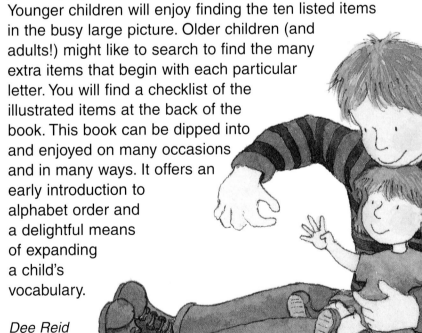

a b c d e f g h i j k l m n o p q r s t u v w x y z

Angry ants, adorable aunts
Angular anchors aweigh
Active acrobats, acorns and apples
Alligators (all A).

acorn
An acre of acorns

ant
A line of angry ants

acrobat
An active acrobat

antelope
The antelope ran up the slope.

alligator
An agitated alligator

apple
A juicy apple

alphabet
I bet you know your alphabet.

arrow
An arrow in a marrow

anchor
The heavy anchor sank her.

astronaut
An astronaut out for a walk.

Aa

See you later alligator.

In a while crocodile.

Use the stepping stones to hop along the alphabet path.

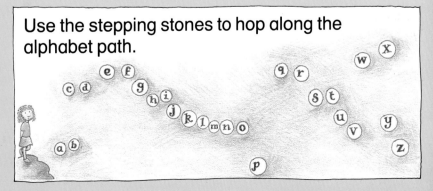

a b c d e f g h i j k l m n o p q r s t u v w x y z

Say 'Hello' to Bill Buffalo
On his bicycle there.
Best balancer in the business
Better than any bear.

baby
A bouncing baby

bicycle
Can you ride a bicycle?

badger
Don't badger a badger.

boat
You can float in a boat.

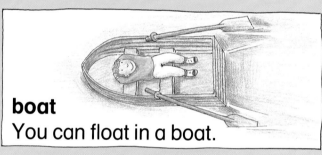

balloon
The balloon popped.

bulldozer
A bulldog in a bulldozer

bear
A hairy bear

bus
A double-decker bus

bee
Buzzing bees

butterfly
A butterfly fluttered by.

Bb

What do you call a sleeping bull?

A bulldozer.

Use the **b** in the balloon to make some words.

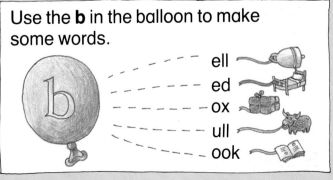

- ell
- ed
- ox
- ull
- ook

a b c d e f g h i j k l m n o p q r s t u v w x y z

Take a bow, cow. Why?
Without you cornflakes would be too dry
Coffee and cocoa undrinkable
Imagine a world without moo-cows? Unthinkable.

camel
A camel with a camera

clock
An alarm clock

camera
A video camera

clown
A clumsy clown

car
A racing car

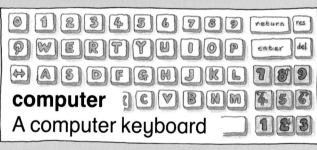

computer
A computer keyboard

castle
A spooky castle

cow
How now brown cow?

caterpillar
A caterpillar with a catapult

crab
A crab might grab you.

Cc

How do you count cows?

With a cowculator.

Find homes for these things that begin with **c**:

cat
cow
canary
car
caterpillar

a b c d e f g h i j k l m n o p q r s t u v w x y z

Two identical dentists sharing a surgery
One called Dennis, the other Sammy
Dennis likes his doughnuts sugary
Sammy, jammy.

daffodil
Daffodils grew on the hills.

dolphin
A diving dolphin

dentist
Two identical dentists

donkey
'Hee-haw,' says the donkey.

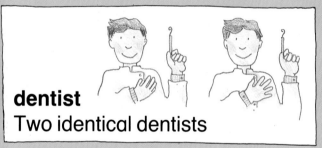

dinosaur
Diplodocus (dip-*plod*-o-kuss)

dragon
A fire-breathing dragon

dog
Does a dog yap in your lap?

drum
Beat the drum.

doll
A doll in a doll's pram

duck
'Quack, quack, come back,'
said mother duck.

Dd

When is it time to see the dentist?

2.30

Can you match the rhyming pairs?

dog   big
dice   lock
door   mice
dock   log
dig   floor

a b c d e f g h i j k l m n o p q r s t u v w x y z

They are building an escalator
Up Mount Everest they say
So that mountaineers like us
Can conquer it each day.

eagle
An eagle in its eyrie

engine
A car engine

ear
You hear with your ears.

envelope
A letter in an envelope

eel
As slippery as an eel

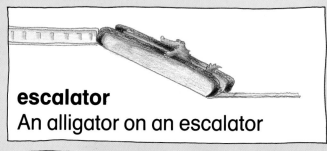

escalator
An alligator on an escalator

egg
Would you expect
an egg to explode?

exit
An extra exit

elephant
Eleven elephants

eye
I saw his eye was sore.

Ee 11

Why do elephants have trunks?

They'd look funny with suitcases, wouldn't they?

A ewe is a mother sheep. Find babies for each of these mothers:

cow   duck   cat   frog

a b c d e f g h i j k l m n o p q r s t u v w x y z

Do you know where factories come from?
They are manufactured intact
Made in Factory factories
As a matter of fact.

factory
A toy factory

flowers
A bunch of flowers

feather
A bird wears its feathers
in all weathers.

fox
The fox slept in its hole.

fire engine
The fire engine's siren wailed.

frog
A freckled frog on a lily leaf.

fish
Wish for a fish on your dish.

fruit
Some fruit in a boot

flag
Would you wag a flag
or let it sag?

frying pan
Six sizzling sausages
in a frying pan

Ff

What do frogs drink?

Croaka Cola.

Can you find which flags match?
Which is the odd one out?

a b c d e f g h i j k l m n o p q r s t u v w x y z

Guy the gorilla played guitar
And wanted to be a superstar
So he formed a group with a goat and a gnu
You can hear them nightly at the zoo.

garage
A large garage.

goat
A goat in a boat.

gate
A squeaky gate.

goldfish
Three goldfish in a bowl.

giraffe
A giraffe in the bath.

gorilla
A gorilla at the tiller.

gloves
A pair of gloves.

grass
The green grass grows.

glue
Gummy glue will stick to you.

guitar
An electric guitar

Gg

Why are goldfish orange?

Because the water makes them rusty.

Tell the story of The Gingerbread Boy

1.
2.
3.
4.
5.
6.

a b c d e f g h i j k l m n o p q r s t u v w x y z

Here comes a hamster with a hammer
Hide the nail
The last time he played handyman
He hurt his tail.

hammer
A hammer and nails

helmet
A fireman's helmet

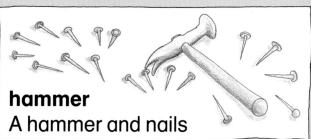

hamster
A hamster in a cage

hippopotamus
A happy hippo

harp
A carp playing the harp

house
A house for a mouse

hedgehog
A tickly, prickly hedgehog

hovercraft
The hovercraft
laughed at the raft.

helicopter
A rescue helicopter

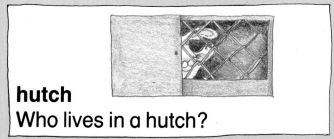

hutch
Who lives in a hutch?

Hh

What do you get when you cross a giraffe with a hedgehog?

An 11 metre hairbrush.

Humpty Dumpty sat on a had a great fall.
All the King's and all the King's
Couldn't put together again.

a b c d e f g h i j k l m n o p q r s t u v w x y z

There is an inkstain on the iceberg
Which means someone has been there
Writing inspiring verses
A poetic polar bear ?

ice
It's nice to see mice on the ice.

iguana
An iguana eating a banana

iceberg
I spy an iceberg.

ink
A bottle of ink

ice cream
Chocolate ice cream

insect
I expect you can
inspect an insect.

icicle
I see an icicle on my tricycle.

island
I land on an island.

igloo
Can you glue an igloo?

ivy
I've an ivy on my wall.

Ii

Knock, knock.

Who's there?

Felix.

Felix who?

Felix my ice cream, I'll lick his.

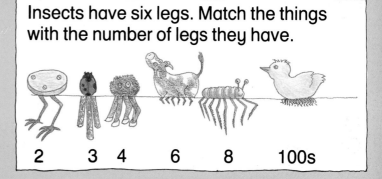

Insects have six legs. Match the things with the number of legs they have.

2   3   4   6   8   100s

a b c d e f g h i j k l m n o p q r s t u v w x y z

A juggler from Jarrow called Klug
Could juggle with a chinaware jug,
Cheap jewellery, jam jars and jigsaws,
Orange jelly and a Japanese mug.

jacket
A leather jacket

jigsaw
Jim saw a jigsaw.

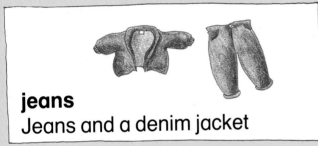

jeans
Jeans and a denim jacket

jockey
A jockey playing hockey

jellyfish
A jellyfish on a smelly dish

judge
A jolly jumping judge

jet
Get a jet to Japan.

jug
A jug and a mug on a rug

jewellery
A jewellery box

juggler
Can a juggler juggle with a jug?

Jj

What jam can't you put on your bread?

toot

beep   honk

A traffic jam.

Here is a jigsaw puzzle. Fit the pieces together to make some farmyard friends.

p   d   en   og

c   h   ig   ow

a b c d e f g h i j k l m n o p q r s t u v w x y z

The kangaroo is the king of karate
(His belt is black)
Kicking quarrelsome kids at a party
(They'll not come back.)

kangaroo
The kangaroo has lost his shoe.

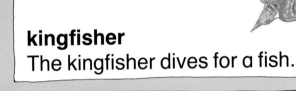

kingfisher
The kingfisher dives for a fish.

kennel
Who sleeps in this kennel?

kitten
Can you count the kittens?

key
He kept the key in the ketchup.

knife
Who knows where a knight
keeps his knife?

kilt
He spilt his milk on his kilt.

knitting
The kitten was sitting
on the knitting.

king
The king wore a ring.

koala
Carla kept a koala in the parlour.

Kk

What's this?

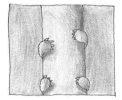

A koala climbing up a tree.

Help the kangaroo to jump along the number path.

(2) (6) (9)

(1) (4) (7) (10)

(3) (5) (8)

Can you do it backwards?

a b c d e f g h i j k l m n o p q r s t u v w x y z

'What is wrong with the rungs on a ladder,'
Said the lady with a leaden frown,
'Is that although there are lots for climbing
There are too few for coming down.'

ladder
An adder had a ladder.

leopard
A leopard who is hiding.

lake
Can you bake a cake on a lake?

lifeboat
Launch the lifeboat.

lamb
A lamb on wobbly legs

lighthouse
A lighthouse on a hill

leaves
In autumn the leaves
leave the trees.

lion
I wouldn't lie on a lion.

lemonade
A litre of lemonade

lollipop
A lollipop in a shop

LI

Why couldn't the leopard escape from the zoo?

Because he was always spotted.

Which one has the most spots?

Which has the fewest?

a b c d e f g h i j k l m n o p q r s t u v w x y z

Monkeying around in a garage
A monkey one midsummer day
Tinkered with a motorbike engine
Which roared and took him away.

magician
A magnificent magician

mirror
See your reflection in the mirror.

magpie
A magpie stole a magnet.

mole
A mole in a mole hole

map
A treasure map

monkey
A cheeky monkey

menu
When you choose from the
menu, choose for me and you.

mouse
One mouse in a house.
Two mice eating rice.

milk
A milk shake

motorbike
I'd like a motorbike.

Mm

What do mice do in the daytime?

Mousework.

What words can the magician make with his magic **m**?

op
an
at
ix
ud

a b c d e f g h i j k l m n o p q r s t u v w x y z

Nettles sting if you fall on them
(It's their way of saying 'How do you do?')
Better ring if you call on them
And only shake hands with your shoe.

nail
Don't fail to hit the nail.

nettle
A stinging nettle

neck
Is your knee next to your neck?

newspaper
A daily newspaper

necklace
A gold necklace

nightingale
A nightingale sings at night.

needle
Do you need a needle?

nurse
A nurse lost her purse.

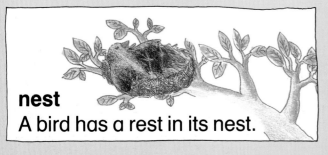

nest
A bird has a rest in its nest.

nut
A squirrel cracking nuts

Nn 9 ♪

What's the difference between a nail and an unlucky boxer?

One's knocked in and the other's knocked out.

Which bird belongs to which nest?

eagle

house martin

blackbird

penguin

a b c d e f g h i j k l m n o p q r s t u v w x y z

A lot of otters wearing overalls
As hot as oven gloves
Trot off down to the river
Which is what an otter loves.

oak
An oak tree is taller than me.

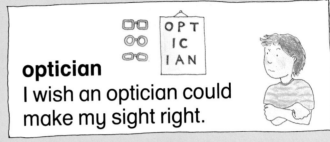

optician
I wish an optician could
make my sight right.

oar
Paddle with a paddle or an oar.

orange
An orange is orange
but this melon is lemon.

oats
Goats eat oats.

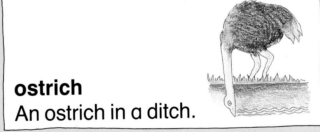

ostrich
An ostrich in a ditch.

ocean
Does the motion of the ocean
make you ill?

otter
The otter has a lotta fun!

oil
I'll oil the engine.

owl
How'll the owl use a towel?

Oo

What do you get if you cross an owl with a skunk?

A bird that smells but doesn't give a hoot.

Can you make all these words from the letters on the octopus' legs?

red   bed   bear
ear   cat   rat
bat   dot   rot

How many more can you make?

a b c d e f g h i j k l m n o p q r s t u v w x y z

Hiccup, Hiccup, Hiccup,
Goes the prickly porcupine
Supine after a super supper
Of pickles, pork pies and port wine.

panda
A panda and a gander

pelican
An American pelican

parachute
A parakeet in a parachute

pencil
Draw around a stencil
with a pencil.

parrot
The parrot pecked a carrot.

pineapple
A piece of pickled pineapple.

peach
Have a peach each.

pirate
Would you fire at a pirate?

peacock
As proud as a peacock

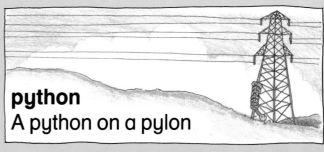

python
A python on a pylon

Pp

What do porcupines eat with cheese?

Prickled onions.

Can you copy like a parrot? Point to the matching words.

Goodbye
Hello
Pretty boy
Got any food?
Let me out

Got any food?
Hello
Goodbye
Pretty boy
Let me out

a b c d e f g h i j k l m n o p q r s t u v w x y z

Hey diddle diddle, here is a riddle
To puzzle out if you can.
What is found in a river (and ends in shiver)
Ring o'roses, red noses and Gran?

queen
The queen quickly asked a question.

rake
Can you make a cake with a rake?

queue
A queue for the boat

rhinoceros
A rhinoceros seems big to us.

quilt
A patchwork quilt

robin
A robin bobbing up and down

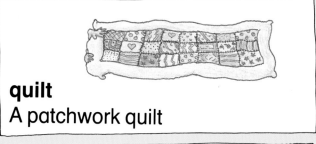

rabbit
A rabbit is nibbling a radish.

robot
Robert the robot

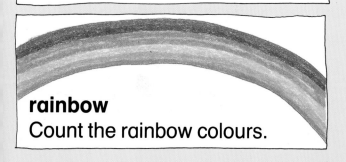

rainbow
Count the rainbow colours.

roller boots
Roll along on roller boots.

Qq Rr

What did the robot say to the petrol pump?

Take your finger out of your ear when I'm talking to you.

The baby rabbit has got lost in his burrow. Which tunnel leads to his mother?

a b c d e f g h i j k l m n o p q r s t u v w x y z

Don't go sliding on the ice in your slippers
It's so slippery that certainly you'll slip
Put on a penguin suit and flippers
To be sure that you get the perfect grip.

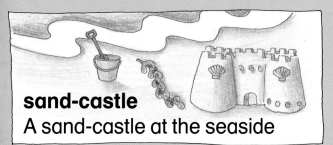

sand-castle
A sand-castle at the seaside

skateboard
A skunk on a skateboard

sausage
A sausage in a saucepan

snail
A snail's silvery trail

scarecrow
A tattered and torn scarecrow

spider
I spied a spider.

seagull
Can you see a seagull?

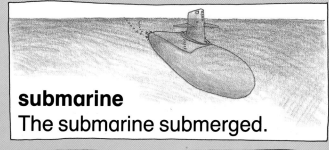

submarine
The submarine submerged.

sheep
Seven shaggy sheep
should be shorn.

swing
Will a king sing on a swing?

Ss

Tongue Twister:

The sixth sick sheik's sixth sheep's sick.

Can you find ten seaside things hidden in the seaweed?

a b c d e f g h i j k l m n o p q r s t u v w x y z

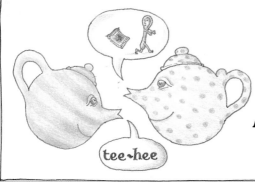

Don't put two teapots together
They will tittle ~ tattle like mad
About tea things like teabags and teaspoons
And the wonderful teatimes they had.

tee~hee

taxi
Elephants need a maxi taxi.

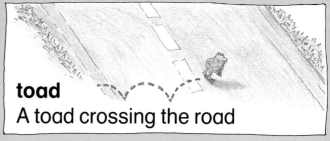

toad
A toad crossing the road

teddy bear
The teddy bear has lost its hair.

tractor
He backed the tractor up the hill.

telephone
A teeny-tiny tortoise
is on the telephone.

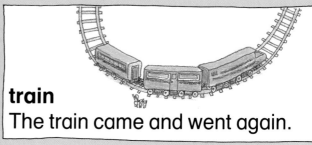

train
The train came and went again.

television
Cartoons on the television

tree
Can you see the bee in the tree?

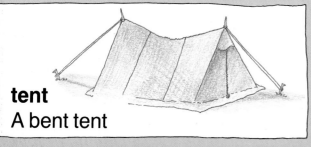

tent
A bent tent

tricycle
You could try a tricycle if you
fall off a bicycle.

Tt

What's yellow and white and travels at over 100 mph?

A train driver's egg sandwich.

Use the typewriter to type these words:

tap   tin   ten   top   tug   tea

a b c d e f g h i j k l m n o p q r s t u v w x y z

While a vulture plays the violin
To a vicar on a verandah
A unicorn blows its horn
And dances with a panda.

umbrella
Tell her to sell her umbrella.

vet
I bet a vet could get a pet.

unicorn
A unicorn has a magic horn.

video
Cartoons on video

uniform
A uniform can keep you warm.

violin
What a din from the violin.

vase
A vase of various violets

volcano
A vole on a volcano

vegetable
A vegetable on the table

vulture
A vulture and a viper on a van

Uu Vv

What goes up when the rain comes down?

An umbrella.

A vet helps sick animals. What jobs do these people do?

a b c d e f g h i j k l m n o p q r s t u v w x y z

How much wood does it take to make a woodpecker?

How many walnuts are there in a wall?

Can a winkle wink? A wombat bat?

Does wearing wellies make you well? (That's all!)

watch
She lost her watch.

windmill
A windmill on a hill

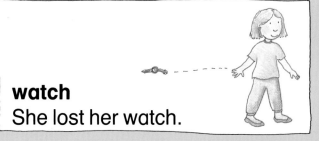

water
The porter brought the water for his daughter.

wood
Would wood taste good?

wheel
We'll wheel the wheel to the wall.

woodpecker
Would a woodpecker peck wood?

wheelbarrow
A sparrow in a wheelbarrow

wool
We wound some white wool.

whistle
Can you whistle on a thistle?

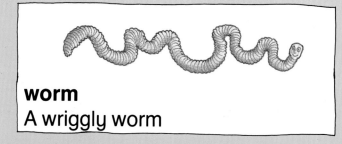

worm
A wriggly worm

Ww

How do worms fall over?

With great difficulty.

Match the wheels with the vehicles:

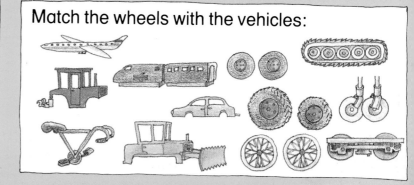

a b c d e f g h i j k l m n o p q r s t u v w x y z

'Yuk!' says the yak, 'it tastes like spam,
Mother's home-made yellow yam jam.'
An ox exclaimed, 'Please give me a pot
The zebras at the zoo will soon scoff the lot.'

X-ray
He examined the
X-ray excitedly.

yoghurt
Yoghurt is yummy.

xylophone
A xylophone makes
a ringing tone.

yo-yo
Have a go-go on my yo-yo.

yacht
Have you got a yacht?

zebra
Debra the zebra

yak
A yak in a mac

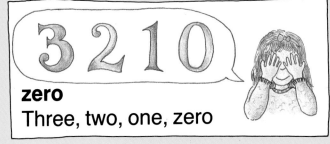
zero
Three, two, one, zero

yellow
The yellow yolk of an egg

zoo
See a gnu at the zoo.

Xx Yy Zz

What is yellow and very dangerous?

Shark infested custard.

Match the footprints with the correct colour.

yellow
red
blue
green
orange

Did you find all these objects in the big pictures?

A
abacus
ace
adder
admiral
aerial
aeroplane
albatross
alien
ambulance
angler
antimacassar
antlers
ape
apricot
aquaduct
aqualung
aquarium
arch
archery
arm
armadillo
artichoke
artist
awning
axe

B
baby
basket
bat
beard
bell
binoculars
blanket
bluebell
bone
book
boomerang
bottle
box
boy
bread
bridge
bulrush
burrow
butter

C
cable
cactus
cage
cake
calculator
calendar
canary
cape
cards
casters
catapult
cauliflower
chain
chair
chandelier
chess
chicken
children
chimpanzee
claw
clogs
cloud

cobweb
cockerel
coffee jug
cogs
colander
comb
confetti
conjuror
cormorant
cot
crane
crate
crocodile
crocus
crow
cuckoo clock
cucumber
cuff
cup
curlers
curtains

D
daffodil
dartboard
darts
deckchair
delicatessen
designer
dice
d.i.y.
doctor
dominoes
double bass
doughnut
dove
drain
draughts
drawing board
drill
drink
dungarees

E
ear-ring
earth
eclair
Egyptian
electric bulb
elf
elk
elm
Ely
embroidery
emerald
emu
entrance
engineer
equator
Evesham
Exmouth
express
extinguisher

F
face
fan
farm
February
fence
ferret

ferry
film
finger
finger-print
fir
fireman
fireworks
fish fingers
five
flame
flamingo
flask
flats
flour
flowers
football
forget-me-not
fork
forklift truck
fountain
French windows
Friday
fruit
funnel

G
gas
gasket
geranium
gerbil
gherkin
ghost
giant
gingerbread man
glasses
glider
gnu
goggles
golf
gooseberry jam
grapefruit
grease
green paint
greenhouse
grill
guide
gum

H
hacksaw
hair
hairbrush
hair-dryer
hamburger
hand
handbag
handcuffs
handkerchief
hare
harmonica
high chair
hive
honey
hoof
hook
horn
horseshoe
hose
house
hyacinth

I
ice cubes
ice skates
illustrator
infant
instrument
ironing board

J
jackal
jackdaw
jack-in-a-box
jam tarts
jelly babies
jelly beans
jester
jet
jewellery
jogger
joke book
judo
juice
juke box
jump

K
kid
kilt
kiss
kitchen
knapsack
knee
knickers
knob
knot

L
label
lace
laces
ladle
lamp
lantern
leap-frog
lemonade
lens
letter
lettuce
library
life-jacket
lightning
lilies
log
look-out
lorry
luggage

M
macaw
mackintosh
magazine
magnifying glass
magnolia
maid
mail-box
maize
man
mandarin
mandolin
marbles
marigold
marmalade
Martian

mashed potato
mask
mast
match
mattress
measles
medal
medicine
melon
meringue
microscope
money
moose
moth
mouse-trap
moustache
muesli
multiplication
mushroom
mussels

N
narcissus
nasturtium
net
netball
nib
nine
North
November
nozzle
nutmeg

O
oboe
observatory
omelette
orbit
organ
origami
outboard motor
oven
oyster

P
pail
paint
paintbrush
palette
palm tree
pansy
panther
parasol
patchwork
path
pear
pen
penny farthing
perch
periscope
photo
picnic basket
pie
pillow
plait
polar bear
pony-tail
poodle
porcupine
postman
potty

puddle
puffin
Punch and Judy
puppet
pushchair
pyramid

Q
quintuplets

R
raincoat
rattle
recorder
Red Riding Hood
reindeer
reins
rhubarb
ribbon
rock
rocket
rope
rose bush
roundabout
rubbish bin
rucksack
ruler

S
sailboat
sailor
sand
sandals
sandwich
scarf
scooter
screw
screwdriver
sea anemone
sea urchin
seal
seaweed
shark
shell
shoes
shorts
shower
sign
sketchbook
sky
snorkel
snowman
socks
spades
spanner
squirrel
starfish
stick
stork
strawberries
string
sun
sun-hat
sun-umbrella
surfboard
swan
swimmer
swimsuit

T
table
tambourine
tangerine

tapes
tea
teacup
tea-tray
tennis ball
tennis racket
thesaurus
thimble
thread
tie
tiger
tights
tinsel
toadstool
toast
toboggan
tomato
tongs
toothpaste
torch
track
trout
trunk
turkey
typewriter

U
vanilla ice-cream
vest

V
video camera
viewing gallery
vine

W
waistcoat
waitress
walrus
wallpaper
wand
wardrobe
washing
washing line
waterfall
watering can
waterlily
wave
weasel
web
wedding
wellington boots
Wendy House
wheelchair
whiskers
wicker basket
wings
wizard
wolf
woman
woollen jumper
woolly hat

X
yawn
yoga

Y
Zeno

Z
zeppelin
zip
Zodiac
zoom
zzzz

How many more can you find?

123 Parents' notes

Small children always enjoy simple number rhymes and games, and these provide excellent preparation for number work once school begins. The two sections that follow develop different aspects of counting.

In the first section we have collected together traditional and modern rhymes and songs dealing with the numbers from 1 to 10, along with counting jokes and quizzes, and number friezes. The rest of the book is devoted to rhymes that introduce children to counting in sequence.

You may have to help with the reading or singing of these rhymes to begin with, but your child will soon start to join in. Children learn best when they are having fun, So, if you both see this book as something to enjoy, the learning can be left to look after itself.

Nicholas Tucker

2 3 4 5 6 7 8 9 10

The one and only. One.
One single and alone.
Is it lonely? Is it proud?
Standing on its own.

Roger McGough

Diddle diddle dumpling my son John,
Went to bed with his trousers on,
One shoe off and one shoe on,
Diddle diddle dumpling my son John.

Hickory dickory dock
The mouse ran up the clock.
The clock struck one;
The mouse ran down,
Hickory dickory dock.

One old orang-utan observing the open ocean.

Can you find all of these?

1 crab
1 sandcastle
1 spade
1 bucket
1 beachball

one-man band

What did the big hand say to the little hand?

I'll be back in one hour.

one-piece

1 2 3 4 5 6 7 8 9 10

Two swans a-swimming
In the warm summer air.
Up the river, down the river,
2 is company. 2 is a pair.

Roger McGough

Two little boats are on the sea,
All is calm as calm can be.
Gently the wind begins to blow,
Two little boats rock to and fro.
Loudly the wind begins to shout,
Two little boats are tossed about.
Gone is the wind, the storm, the rain,
Two little boats sail on again.

Two little eyes to look around,
Two little ears to hear each sound;
One little nose to smell what's sweet,
One little mouth that likes to eat.

Two tiny teddy bears tasting treacle tarts at tea time.

Can you find these pairs?

salt and pepper
oranges and lemons
strawberries and cream

bread and butter
fish and chips
beans and toast

two-seater

Why did the elephant take two trunks on holiday?

One to drink with, the other to swim in.

two by two

1 2 3 4 5 6 7 8 9 10

Three is a crowd.(But only just.)
I'll tell you a secret if I must.
When I open my eyes what do I see?
Three is Teddy, Bunny and me.

Roger McGough

Three little ghosties
Sitting on three posties
Eating buttered toasties
Sucking their fisties
Right up to their wristies
Weren't they little beasties?

Wire, briar, limber, lock;
Three geese in a flock.
One flew east,
One flew west,
And one flew over
    the cuckoo's nest.

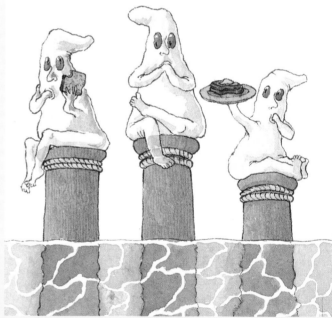

Three thirsty thrushes threading through the thistles.

How many parcels are in the postbox?
How many birds are in the tree?
How many dogs are in the street?
How many children are playing?
How many dustbins can you see?

three-legged race

Have you heard the story of the three wells?

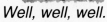

Well, well, well.

three-wheeler

1 2 3 4 5 6 7 8 9 10

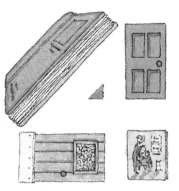

Four corners on a book,
Four corners on the door.
Oh so neat and tidy
(How many letters make four?)

Roger McGough

This morning I counted to four:
When the cat jumped on my bed,
1, 2, 3, 4 legs;
When I had my breakfast,
1, 2, 3, 4 chairs;
When I played with my truck,
1, 2, 3, 4 wheels;
And when I had my sleep,
1, 2, 3, 4 . . . .

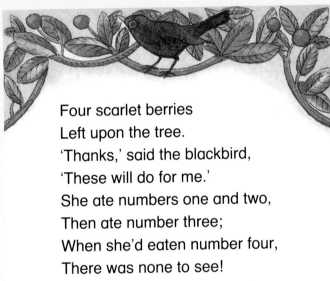

Four scarlet berries
Left upon the tree.
'Thanks,' said the blackbird,
'These will do for me.'
She ate numbers one and two,
Then ate number three;
When she'd eaten number four,
There was none to see!

Four fat floppy frogs flipping from the freezing fountain.

Can you find all of these?

4 furry toys
4 toys with wheels
4 noisy toys
4 toys you would like to play with

four-leaved clover

What has four legs and can't walk?

A bed.

going on all fours

1 2 3 4 5 6 7 8 9 10

Five is your hands favourite number,
Count each finger on your nose.
If that was easy, lift your foot
And try again with your toes.

Roger McGough

Five little monkeys walked along the shore;
One went a-sailing,
Then there were four.

Four little monkeys climbed up a tree;
One of them tumbled down,
Then there were three.

Three little monkeys found a pot of glue;
One got stuck in it,
Then there were two.

Two little monkeys found a currant bun;
One ran away with it,
Then there was one.

One little monkey cried all afternoon,
So they put him in an aeroplane
And sent him to the moon.

Five little squirrels sat up in a tree,
The first one said, 'What do I see?'
The second one said, 'A man with a gun.'
The third one said, 'Then we'd better run.'
The fourth one said, 'Let's hide in the shade.'
The fifth one said, 'I'm not afraid.'
Then **bang** went the gun, and how they did run.

Five furry fox cubs fearlessly frisking through fields and forests.

These five animal babies are looking for their mothers. Can you see where each one should go?

five senses

seeing
hearing
smelling
tasting
touching

What do you call five bottles of lemonade?

A pop group.

1 2 3 4 5 6 7 8 9 10

Six hisses like a serpent,
Six kisses mean a lot.
A yoyo dancing on a string
Trick cyclist balancing on the spot.

Roger McGough

Six little mice sat down to spin,
Pussy passed by, and she peeped in.
'What are you doing, my little men?'
'Weaving coats for gentlemen.'
'May I come in, and cut off your threads?'
'Oh no, Mistress Pussy, you'll bite off our heads!'
'Oh no, I'll not. I'll help you to spin.'
'That may be so, but you can't come in.'

Insects have six legs, no more,
But nobody is really sure
That all those legs are legs not arms.

Maybe they have three of each,
Or four and two, or two and four.

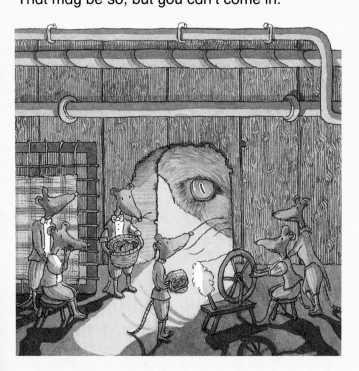

No, nobody is really sure,
When knitting socks for insects.

Six shaggy sheep scampering skilfully in scarlet socks.

These children do not know how to behave in the countryside. Can you see six things they are doing wrong?

1 dropping litter **4** chasing the animals
2 leaving the gate open **5** stealing birds' eggs
3 picking wild flowers **6** lighting a fire

six of hearts

When does a horse have six legs?

When it's got a rider on its back.

half a dozen eggs

1 2 3 4 5 6 7 8 9 10

Seven points the way ahead,
Like a policeman, arm out straight.
Gives direction, sharp and sensible,
Unlike its neighbour, number eight.

Roger McGough

As I was going to St Ives,
I met a man with seven wives.
Each wife had seven sacks,
Each sack had seven cats,
Each cat had seven kits,
Kits, cats, sacks and wives,
How many were going to St Ives?

One - yourself!

I saw seven magpies in a tree

Two for you and five for me:

One for sorrow, two for joy,

Three for a girl, and four for a boy;

Five for silver, six for gold,

shhhhhhh . . . .

Seven for a secret never to be told.

Seven skipping schoolchildren singing silly songs.

Can you find seven things these children are doing at school?

1 painting
2 reading
3 writing
4 cutting out

5 modelling
6 measuring
7 singing

seven days of the week

What is furry and has fourteen legs?

Seven teddy bears.

1 2 3 4 5 6 7 8 9 10

Eight is a fat cat. Balancing doughnuts.
A pair of goggles on its side.
A figure of eight a roller coaster
Take your finger for a ride.

Roger McGough

One, two, three, four,
Mary at the cottage door.
Five, six, seven, eight,
Eating cherries off a plate.

Eight babies laughing loud, eight babies singing.

Seven babies clapping hands, one baby ringing.

Six babies banging drums, two babies rattling.

Five babies dancing high, three babies chattering.

Four babies drinking juice, four babies feeding.

Eight babies ready for bed, eight babies sleeping.

Eight excited elephants enjoying an expedition.

Can you spot these eight animals?

parrot	anteater
monkey	bat
toucan	sloth
snake	lizard

figure of eight

What eight-letter word has only one letter in it?

An envelope.

Henry VIII

1 2 3 4 5 6 7 8 9 10

Nine walks tall, puffs out its chest.
Happily banging a big bass drum.
Can you count how many times?
Tum-pity. Tum-pity. Tum, Tum, Tum.

Roger McGough

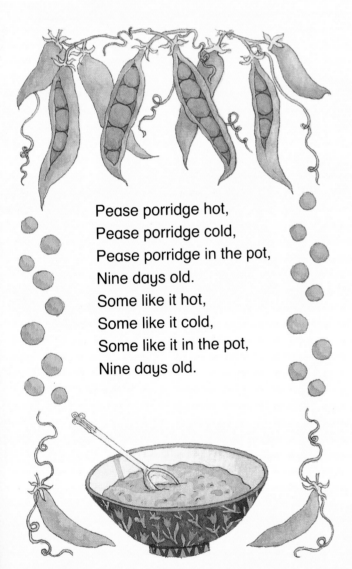

Pease porridge hot,
Pease porridge cold,
Pease porridge in the pot,
Nine days old.
Some like it hot,
Some like it cold,
Some like it in the pot,
Nine days old.

I'll sing you a song,
Nine verses long,
For a pin:
Three and three are six
And three are nine;
You are a fool,
And the pin is mine.

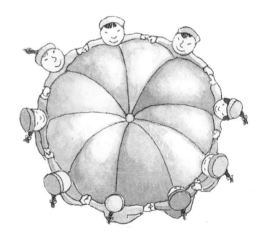

Nine nesting nightingales nibbling nuts in the nippy New Year.

There are nine snowflakes hidden in this picture. Can you find them?

ninepins

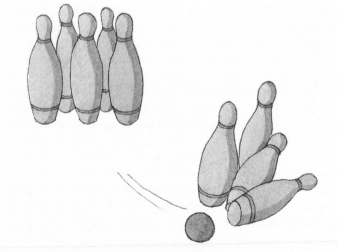

If I had four snowballs in my right hand and five in my left, what would I have?

Cold hands.

1 2 3 4 5 6 7 8 9 10

Ten looks really grown-up
(One at last has found a friend)
Ten has lots of tricks to show you
For numbers are fun without end.

Roger McGough

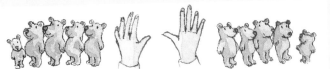

Ten little teddy bears stand up straight,

Ten little teddy bears make a gate,

Ten little teddy bears make a ring,

Ten little teddy bears bow to the king.

Ten little teddy bears dance all day,

Ten little teddy bears hide away.

Cluck, cluck, cluck, cluck.
Good morning, Mrs Hen.
How many chicks have you got?
Madam, I've got ten,
Four of them are yellow,
Four of them are brown,
And two of them are speckled red,
The nicest in the town.

Ten turquoise teapots teetering on the tray.

Mrs Harris went to Paris. She bought a ⬮, an ⬮, a ⬮, a ⬮, a ⬮, a ⬮, a ⬮, an ⬮, a ⬮ and a ⬮.

How many things did Mrs Harris buy?

ten fingers

If Mrs Harris cuts her orange into four pieces and her banana into six pieces, what will she get?

Fruit salad.

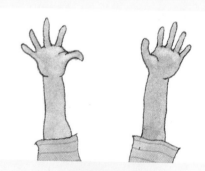

ten toes

One, two, three,
Mother caught a flea.
Put it in the teapot,
And made a cup of tea.

One, two, three, four, five,
Once I caught a fish alive.
Six, seven, eight, nine, ten,
Then I let it go again.

Why did I let it go?
Because it bit my finger so.
Which finger did it bite?
This little finger on my right.

This old man, he played one,
He played nick-nack on my drum.

With a nick-nack, paddy wack,
Give a dog a bone.
This old man went rolling home.

This old man, he played two,
He played nick-nack on my shoe.

With a nick-nack, paddy wack . . .

This old man, he played three,
He played nick-nack on my knee.

This old man, he played four,
He played nick-nack on my door.

This old man, he played five,
He played nick-nack on my hive.

This old man, he played six,
He played nick-nack on my sticks.

This old man, he played seven,
He played nick-nack up in heaven.

This old man, he played eight,
He played nick-nack on my gate.

This old man, he played nine,
He played nick-nack on my line.

This old man, he played ten,
He played nick-nack on my hen.

The animals went in one by one,
The elephant chewing a caraway bun.

The animals went in two by two,
The rhinoceros and the kangaroo.

The animals went in three by three,
The wasp, the flea and the bumble bee.

The animals went in four by four,
The great hippopotamus stuck in the door.

The animals went in five by five,
With great big trunks they did arrive.

The animals went in six by six,
The hyena laughed at the monkeys' tricks.

The animals went in seven by seven,
Said the ant to the elephant, 'Who are you shoving?'

The animals went in eight by eight,
The worm was early, the bird was late.

The animals went in nine by nine,
Some had water and some had wine.

The animals went in ten by ten,
If you want any more you must sing it again.
And they all went into the Ark,
For to get out of the rain.

One, two,
Buckle my shoe.
Three, four,
Knock at the door.
Five, six,
Pick up sticks.
Seven, eight,
Lay them straight.
Nine, ten,
A big fat hen.
Eleven, twelve,
Dig and delve.
Thirteen, fourteen,
Maids a-courting.
Fifteen, sixteen,
Maids in the kitchen.
Seventeen, eighteen,
Maids in waiting.
Nineteen, twenty,
My plate's empty.

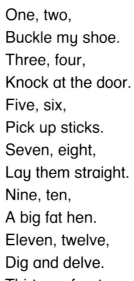

One, two, kittens that mew,
Two, three, birds on a tree,
Three, four, shells on the shore,
Four, five, bees in the hive,
Five, six, the cow that licks,
Six, seven, rooks in the heaven,
Seven, eight, sheep at the gate,
Eight, nine, clothes on the line,
Nine, ten, the little black hen.

On the first day of Christmas
My true love sent to me
A partridge in a pear tree.

On the second day of Christmas
My true love sent to me
Two turtle doves and
A partridge in a pear tree.

On the third day of Christmas
My true love sent to me
Three French hens . . .

On the fourth day of Christmas
My true love sent to me
Four calling birds . . .

On the fifth day of Christmas
My true love sent to me
Five gold rings . . .

On the sixth day of Christmas
My true love sent to me
Six geese a-laying . . .

On the seventh day of Christmas
My true love sent to me
Seven swans a-swimming...

On the eighth day of Christmas
My true love sent to me
Eight maids a-milking...

On the ninth day of Christmas
My true love sent to me
Nine drummers drumming...

On the tenth day of Christmas
My true love sent to me
Ten pipers piping...

On the eleventh day of Christmas
My true love sent to me
Eleven ladies dancing...

On the twelfth day of Christmas
My true love sent to me
Twelve lords a-leaping...

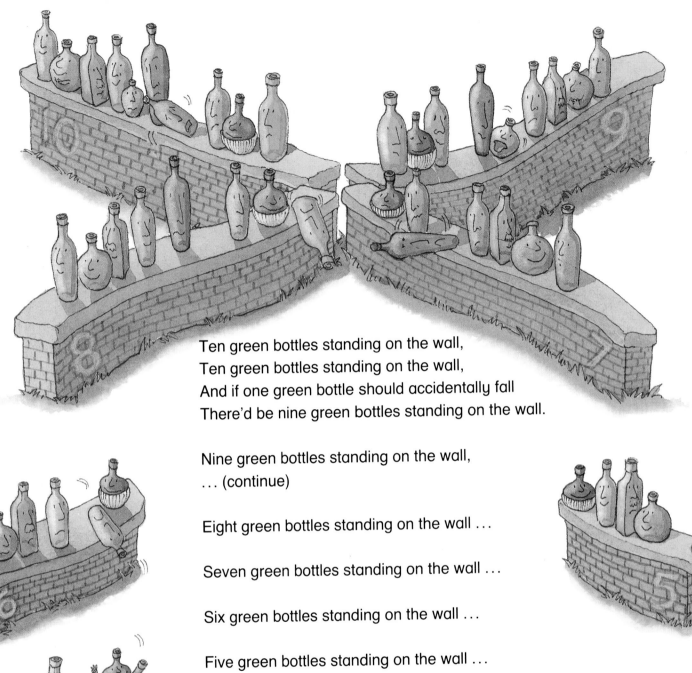

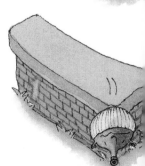

Ten green bottles standing on the wall,
Ten green bottles standing on the wall,
And if one green bottle should accidentally fall
There'd be nine green bottles standing on the wall.

Nine green bottles standing on the wall,
… (continue)

Eight green bottles standing on the wall …

Seven green bottles standing on the wall …

Six green bottles standing on the wall …

Five green bottles standing on the wall …

Four green bottles standing on the wall …

Three green bottles standing on the wall …

Two green bottles standing on the wall …

One green bottle standing on the wall,
One green bottle standing on the wall,
And if that green bottle should accidentally fall
There'd be no green bottles standing on the wall.

One man went to mow,
Went to mow a meadow;
One man and his dog,
Went to mow a meadow.

Two men went to mow,
Went to mow a meadow;
Two men, one man and his dog,
Went to mow a meadow.

Three men went to mow,
… (continue)

Four men went to mow …

Five men went to mow …

Six men went to mow …

Seven men went to mow …

Eight men went to mow …

Nine men went to mow …

Ten men went to mow …

How many animals are there in each of these groups?
See if you can count them for yourself.

Can you find all these objects in the big picture?

1 beach hut
deckchair
flag
rock pool
seaweed
shells
sunglasses
yacht

How many sandcastles?
How many starfish?

2 bib
breadknife
high chair
jam pot
milk jug
place mat
sugar bowl
teapot

How many forks?
How many knives?
How many spoons?

3 apron
banana
box
door
gate
key
lid
lobster
saddle
sausages
swing

How many baskets?
How many wheels?

4 bear
bucket
doll
drum
giraffe
kite
lion
pig
puppet
rabbit
signal
spider
tractor
trumpet

How many ducks?
How many flowers?

5 canoe
fox
gloves
goose
paddle
penguin
polar bear
scarf
seal

How many animals?
How many children?

6 barbed wire
bird
bluebells
gate
nest
rabbit
sheep
stile

How many bars on the
gate?
How many pieces of litter?

7 castanets
computer
cymbals
newspaper
recorder
rolling pin
scissors
snake
tamborine
tape-measure
triangles

How many children reading
books?
How many paper dolls?
How many colours in a
paintbox?

8 ants
chameleon
explorers
frog
rope ladder

How many butterflies?
How many monkeys?

9 carrot
holly
igloo
scarf
skier
spade
toboggan
tracks

How many deer?
How many mice?

10 How many things did Mrs.
Harris buy to eat?
How many things did she
buy to wear?
How many of her things
would you like to buy?